# Write Fast, Write Funny

## A Guide for Writing Short Humor

by Mike Artell

Illustrated by
Randy Verougstraete,
Michele Episcopo,
and Robert Dobaczewski

Good Apple

Editor: Donna Garzinsky

GOOD APPLE
An Imprint of Modern Curriculum
A Division of Simon & Schuster
299 Jefferson Road, P. O. Box 480
Parsippany, NJ 07054-0480

1 2 3 4 5 6 7 8 9 MAL 01 00 99 98 97

# Contents

# Introduction

Some people can write long, detailed stories that capture and delight the imaginations of their readers. Others (equally talented) are much better at writing short, clever gems that are just as worthy of attention and praise.

*Write Fast, Write Funny* can help develop and encourage those writers interested in writing the short stuff. Although this book emphasizes humor and cleverness, it also focuses on language usage and an understanding of the basics. This is not frivolous work. This is real writing.

To make an effective joke, a person must understand what he or she is joking about. We've all been in situations where someone in a group told a joke and the joke fell flat. Most likely we didn't understand the setup, or premise. People who make jokes successfully usually grasp what they're talking about and can predict their audience's response. This should be an encouragement to teachers and parents whose "class clowns" seem out of touch with what's going on around them. The class clown is making a joke about something he or she relates to, and that understanding can serve as the basis for a deeper knowledge of the subject.

Hi I'm Led

Welcome

# How to Use This Book

*Write Fast, Write Funny* can be used by teachers and parents in many ways. Here are just a few.

## As a warm-up for more serious writing exercises

Prior to writing stories, poems, or research papers, the activities in this book can help focus students on the writing task in a fun, kid-friendly way. Since the writing suggestions are generally short, they require just a minimum of classroom time.

## As an activity book to engage a child in a quiet, educational activity

In a car, on a rainy day, or as an alternative to television viewing, the writing suggestions in this book can engage a child in positive and rewarding ways.

## As a tie-in to specific curriculum areas

Writing humorously about specific subjects (such as reptiles, weather, or famous historical figures) is a fresh way to challenge students to express their understanding of the topic and communicate in a way that readers will find interesting.

## As a guidebook that kids can use to create their own humor books

Some children will use this book as a springboard to create their own joke, riddle, and tongue-twister books. For teachers interested in developing young authors and illustrators, this book can help launch students in the direction of humorous writing.

# TERRIFIC TONGUE-TWISTER TECHNIQUES

## Value and Educational Applications

- Familiarity with the nature and use of consonant blends

- Use of proper and common nouns and adjectives

- Sentence construction

- Introduction to alliteration

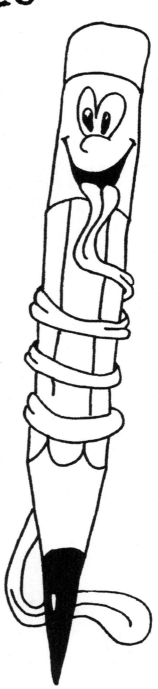

# Writing Technique

There are several kinds of tongue twisters. Regardless of the type, tongue twisters are one of the easiest forms of humor to write. Here's how it's done.

1. Make a list of consonant blends.
   **Examples:** *st fr cl br bl dr fl gr pr pl sn tr*

2. Pick a consonant blend and write it on a piece of paper three times. Leave space between the second and third pairs of consonants.
   **Examples:** *st st    st*
            *fr fr    fr*

3. In the space, write the first consonant of the consonant blend you've chosen, but put a vowel in the place of the second consonant in the blend.
   **Examples:** *st st so st*
            *fr fr fi fr*

4. Choose words to go with each blend.
   **Examples:** *Stephanie's stained socks stink!*
            *Freddy fried fish Friday.*

5. Voilà! You've written a tongue twister. Now make it more complicated by adding additional words.
   **Examples:** *Stephanie Stevens' stained soccer socks stink!*
            *Freddy Freeman fried five fine fish Friday.*

6. Let's create another kind of tongue twister. Instead of changing the beginning of each word, change the middle of each word.

   **Like this:** *Buddy's bully buddies bugged Bonnie Bunny's buddies.*

The trick to writing tongue twisters is to get people's tongues used to repeating a pattern. Then you change the pattern—then go back to the original pattern. Their tongues can't keep up!

# Adding Illustrations

Illustrations add a lot to humorous writing. Here are illustrations for two of the tongue twisters we've just written.

Stephanie Stevens' stained soccer socks stink!

Freddy Freeman fried five fine fish Friday.

Even if you think you can't draw, it's still fun to add some simple illustrations. The idea is to be imaginative with words and pictures, not to create the *Mona Lisa*. Use stick people if you have to, but give it a try!

# Cross-Curriculum Uses

### Science

Create tongue twisters based on various areas of science, such as astronomy (*Seeing seven stars, Stan stared silently*) or biology (*Mr. Mustard's muscles must move Mr. Mustard's mouth*).

### Math

Basic and advanced math concepts can be incorporated into tongue twisters. For example, geometry (*Trina told Tim to try tracing triangles*) or arithmetic (*Square roots scare Ruth*).

### Social Studies

You can base tongue twisters on famous people, objects, places, or events. For example, *Presidents Pierce and Polk probably popped popcorn*, or *Franklin's friends in France found Franklin friendly*.

Look for alliterative or unusual place names that might inspire tongue twisters, such as *Timbuktu; Walla Walla, Washington;* or *Bora Bora*.

### Reading/Language Arts

Invent tongue twisters about plot or personality that are based on unusual or alliterative book titles and character names, such as *Maniac Magee* and *Jumanji*.

### Additional Ideas

• Invite students to write tongue twisters using their names.

• Assign groups of students several letters of the alphabet. Challenge them to write and illustrate tongue twisters that begin with each of their letters.

# WRITING RIDICULOUS RIDDLES

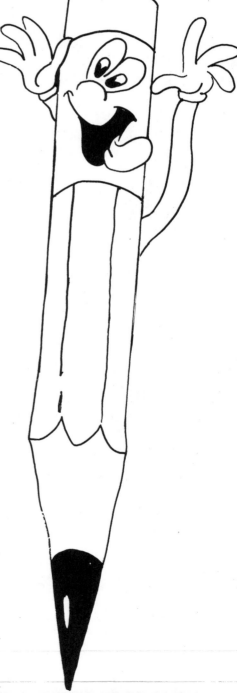

## Value and Educational Applications

- Familiarity with the nature and use of homophones

- Introduction to synonyms

- Creation of playful imagery

# Writing Technique

**Most riddles in riddle books are really plays on homophones.**
**Example:** What kind of deer always carries an umbrella?
     A *rain*deer!

This riddle is a play on the homophones *rein* (in *reindeer*)
and *rain*.

A true riddle is more "deceptive" in its question.
**Example:** Which state is round on both ends and high in
     the middle?
     O-HI-O!

Riddles based on homophones are much easier to write and are
best for young students. To create homophone riddles, look for
words within words or words that sound like other words.

**Examples:** In the word *autographs*, *auto* sounds like "ought to."
     The word *auto* also means "car."

     In the word *catalog*, the first two syllables sound like
     *cattle*. The last syllable sounds like *log*.

Now you need some good questions—the key to good riddles.

**Examples:** How do famous cars sign their names?
     With *auto*graphs!

     Where can you buy presents for cows and horses?
     In a *cattle*log!

# Adding Illustrations

Clever illustrations can add a lot to the riddles. Here's how you might illustrate the riddles we just wrote.

How do famous cars sign
their names?
With *autographs.*

Where can you buy presents
for cows and horses?
In a *cattlelog!*

# Cross-Curriculum Uses

## Science

Have students create a book of ecology or animal riddles. See the bibliography for books that will help you get started. Subjects might include the *desert* (it sounds similar to *dessert*), *rain forest* (*rain* sounds similar to the name *Wayne*), *parrot* (sounds similar to *parent*), and *giraffe* (imagine a giraffe floating on a *gi-raft*).

## Math

Create riddles based on numbers—they don't have to be based on homophones. Here are a few examples: *If two's company and three's a crowd, what's four and five? Nine!  What did the numbers 3 and 5 do on their date? They 8!  Why didn't the numbers 4 and 2 come to school today? They were feeling 6.*

## Reading/Language Arts

Add riddle books to your class library. Encourage students to memorize and recite their favorite riddles. Have students discuss mystery books they have read that contain riddles.

## Social Studies

Create riddles based on countries (Greece and Turkey are obvious choices) or natural features such as rivers and mountain ranges. (See also the suggestions under Science, above.)

## Additional Ideas

Discuss how police detectives often have to solve riddles while investigating a crime or how some Oriental cultures use riddles to encourage deeper thought (*What is the sound of one hand clapping?*). You may wish to have students explore riddles that play off of this ability to think abstractly. For example, *How far can a dog run into a forest? Half way . . . then it's running out of the forest*, or *How long is a piece of string? Twice the distance from one end to the middle.*

# RARE PAIRS

## Value and Educational Applications

- Introduction and use of rhyming words

- Use of synonyms

- Creation of question-and-response dialogue

# Writing Technique

This activity is a great way to introduce younger children or children with limited language skills to humorous writing. The punch lines of Rare Pairs are two words that rhyme. To create a Rare Pair, you need to write a question, or setup, that leads to the rhyming words.

Suppose you've chosen the rhyming pair *big* and *pig*. To write a question with the answer *big pig*, choose a synonym for each word. A synonym for *big* is *large*. A synonym for *pig* is *hog*. Now put the synonyms in the form of a question.

**Example:**   What do you call a large hog?
          A big pig!

Easy, right? Let's use the rhyming words *little* and *fiddle*. A synonym for *little* is *small*. A synonym for *fiddle* is *violin*. Put the synonyms in the form of a question.

**Example:**   What do you call a small violin?
          A little fiddle!

The lists of rhyming pairs in a rhyming dictionary can help students jump-start a Rare Pair. See the bibliography for more information.

What do you call a small violin?
A little fiddle!

# Cross-Curriculum Uses

### Science

Create Rare Pairs for animals (*fat bat, regal eagle, shy fly*) or for plants (*stern fern, lazy daisy, silly lily*).

### Reading/Language Arts

Have students create Rare Pairs for stories and books they are reading.
For example, *Who would represent Huck Finn's friend in court?*
*A Tom Sawyer lawyer!*

### Social Studies

Encourage students to create Rare Pairs for famous people.
For example, *What would you call a famous president who gets smaller and smaller?*
*A shrinkin' Lincoln!*

They can also try inventing geography Rare Pairs.
For example, *What would you call a cold bowl of meat and beans in South America?*
*Chilly Chile Chili!*

# ONE, TWO, VACUUM THE ZOO

## Value and Educational Applications

- Rhythm and rhyming skills

- Introduction and use of meter

- Creative thinking

# Writing Technique

Read aloud the following popular nursery rhyme. Encourage students to share variations they have heard.

> One, two, buckle my shoe.
> Three, four, shut the door.
> Five, six, pick up sticks.
> Seven, eight, lay them straight.
> Nine, ten, a big, fat hen.

To make a *nonsense* rhyme out of it, follow each pair of numbers with a new rhyming phrase.

**Example:**
> One, two, vacuum the zoo.
> Three, four, why do you snore?
> Five, six, my dog does tricks.
> Seven, eight, grandma can skate!
> Nine, ten, bald-headed men.

The rhyme does not have to make sense (grandma can skate?). But there are two basic rules to follow: The last word of each line must rhyme with the second number, and the added phrase must contain three or four syllables. You can be flexible with the rules until your students catch on.

You may wish to help students get started in making their own rhymes by providing them with a rhyming dictionary or the following lists of rhyming words.

"One, two . . ." *atchoo! blue boo chew clue do few flew flu glue grew igloo knew moo new shampoo stew sue threw too who you zoo*

"Three, four . . ." *before door explore floor galore more oar pour roar score shore snore sore store wore*

"Five, six . . ." *bricks chicks clicks fix kicks licks mix picks tricks*

"Seven, eight . . ." *bait date gate great hate late plate skate state wait weight*

"Nine, ten . . ." *again Ben den men pen then when*

You might also try rhyming descending numbers.

**Example:**        Ten, nine, step in line.
Eight, seven, I see Kevin.
Six, five, bees in the hive.
Four, three, look at me.
Two, one, now I'm done.

Reworking this nursery rhyme can be a great cooperative learning exercise for five groups of students. Assign to each group a pair of numbers, ascending or descending. Tell students to create and illustrate original rhymes using their numbers. Display students' work in the classroom.

One, two, vacuum the zoo.

# Cross-Curriculum Uses

### Science

Challenge students to create rhymes based on a science theme.
For example, *One, two, the sea is blue. Three, four, swimmers explore.*

### Math

Create math rhymes using the product, sum, or quotient as the rhyming word. Students may have to bend the rhythm of the poem. For example, *6 times 4 is 24. Now let's do a little more. 6 times 7 is 42. Boy, I'm glad we're almost through!*

### Social Studies

Create rhymes based on the names of countries.
For example, *One, two, where is Peru? Three, four, near Ecuador.*

# "BIG WORD" NURSERY RHYMES

## Value and Educational Applications

- Vocabulary development

- Comprehension and analysis skills

- Dictionary and study skills

# Writing Technique

Most students will enjoy rewriting nursery rhymes. The idea is to replace simple words with fancy synonyms or definitions, using a thesaurus or dictionary. Challenge students to make the nursery rhymes as esoteric as possible, then recite them in a serious tone of voice. Their classmates can try to guess the original rhymes.

Example:    Gently agitate the infant
In the uppermost part of the tree.
When the current of air blows against the bed
    containing the infant,
It will move back and forth.
When the limb holding it breaks,
The bed will drop from the tree,
And the infant and the bed will be affected by gravity.

Did you recognize "Rock-a-bye, Baby"?

Here's an illustration of the first part of this nursery rhyme.

# Cross-Curriculum Uses

## Science/Reading/Language Arts

By substituting "big words" for common words and phrases, students might feel less intimidated when they encounter new scientific or technical terms.

- Students might invent big words using prefixes such as *bio-* and *exo-*. Then they can use their new words in conversations. For example, *Hey, Jason, let's play in the exoenvironment instead of inside.*

- Pencils and other common objects can also be transformed into big words. For example, *Rasheem, may I borrow your cylindrical writing utensil?*

## Additional Ideas

Students may wish to create flashcards with a drawing of an object on one side and a big-word description of the object on the other. After the cards are shuffled with the drawing side down, volunteers can take turns choosing a card, reading the big words, and trying to deduce what the object is. Students can then turn over the card to check their guesses.

# SPOONERISMS

## Value and Educational Applications

- Creative thinking

- Diction and speaking skills

- Increased language usage

# Writing Technique

Spoonerisms are humorous slips of the tongue. They are created by switching the beginning consonant sounds of nearby words. Spoonerisms are named after William Spooner, who was a professor at Oxford University, in England. He lived from 1844 to 1930.

Example:    *Cinderella dropped her slipper* becomes *Rindercella slopped her dripper.*

Here are some ways to use spoonerisms.

1.  Rewrite the titles of fairy tales and nursery rhymes. If your students enjoy making spoonerisms, encourage them to rewrite the entire story or rhyme.

Examples:    "Loldigocks and the Bee Threars"
"Woe Snite and the Deven Swarfs"
"Rittle Led Hiding Rood"
"The Three Gilly Boats Gruff"

2.  Rewrite familiar song titles or lyrics.

Examples:    "Bappy Hirthday You Too"
"Snosty the Froeman"
"Here Comes Keter Pottontail"
"She'll Be Mummin' 'Round the Countin' "

# Cross-Curriculum Uses

### Science

Challenge students to rewrite vocabulary definitions as spoonerisms. For example, *Biology is the study of life* becomes *Biology is the luddy of stife*. *Most mammals are covered with hair* becomes *Most mammals are hovered with care*.

### Reading/Language Arts

Rewrite famous people's names (*Lay Jeno*), movie titles (*Purassic Jark, Gorrest Fump*), book titles (*Boose Gumps*), or sports teams (the *Callas Dowboys*).

### Social Studies

Rewrite famous people's names (*Fenjamin Branklin, Parco Molo*). Write a short biographical sketch of the famous person in a spoonerized style.

# KNOCK-KNOCKS

## Value and Educational Applications

- Use of synonyms

- Creation of question-and-response dialogue

- Creative thinking

- Structural analysis of vocabulary

# Writing Technique

We've all heard knock-knock jokes. Some are funny; some are just painful. Many knock-knocks depend on puns for their humor. You may wish to bring to class some of the knock-knock books listed in the bibliography and use them to discuss plays on words.

Examples:

Knock, knock.
Who's there?
Hatch.
Hatch, who?
Geshundheit!

Knock, knock.
Who's there?
Boo.
Boo, who?
Hey, you don't have to cry about it!

Proper names are good fodder for knock-knocks. Look at proper names and see if you can discover some similar-sounding words within them. Two-syllable words seem to work best.

Examples:

*Barton* . . . Barton *(Pardon)* me, is this seat taken?

*Phillip* . . . Phillip *(Fill up)* my glass with soda please.

*Watson* . . . Watson *(What's in)* that bag you're carrying?

*Desi* . . . Desi *(Does he)* want to go with us?

*Kenny* . . . Kenny *(Can he)* come along?

*Manny* . . . Manny (*Many*) people think you're silly.

*Ella* . . . Ella-phants (*Elephants*) never forget.

*Dewey* . . . Dewey (*Do we*) both have to talk at once?

*Ron* . . . Ron (*Run*) up to the store and buy some milk.

Here are some other words you can use to create knock-knocks.

**Examples:**

*water* . . . Water (*What a*) strange hat you're wearing!

*daylight* . . . Daylight (*They light*) candles when it gets dark.

Words beginning with the letters "*de*" are great for knock-knocks.

**Examples:**

*debate* . . . Debate (*The bait*) has to be on the hook to catch a fish.

*decay* . . . Decay (*The* k) comes between the *j* and the *l*.

*deceive* . . . Deceive (*The sieve*) can be used to strain the liquid.

*decide* . . . Decide (*The side*) pointing toward you looks the best.

*declare* . . . Declare (*The clear*) weather made it easy to see the stars.

*decrease* . . . Decrease (*The grease*) stopped the wheel from squeaking.

*defeat* . . . Defeat (*The feet*) on that clown are huge!

# Cross-Curriculum Uses

## Science

Encourage students to create science knock-knocks.

For example,

> *Knock, knock.*
> *Who's there?*
> *Your aunt.*
> *My aunt who?*
> *Your aunt-phibian! Ribbit! Ribbit!*

## Math

Students can make knock-knock jokes based on various branches of math.

For example,

> *Knock, knock.*
> *Who's there?*
> *Al.*
> *Al who?*
> *Algebra!*

## Additional Ideas

Students may enjoy making knock-knocks based on cultural events.

For example,

> *Knock, knock.*
> *Who's there?*
> *Sue.*
> *Sue who?*
> *Superbowl!*

# IT WAS SO HOT TODAY . . .

## Value and Educational Applications

- Introduction to metaphors, similes, and exaggeration

- Creation of vivid imagery

- Use of synonyms

# Writing Technique

This form of humorous writing contains amusing, ridiculous, or outrageous comparisons. To create the joke, think of normal situations, events, or objects. Then imagine how they might be affected by an extreme condition such as excessive heat, cold, speed, or height.

Example:

*It was so hot today that I saw a dog chasing a cat . . . and they were both walking.*

A dog chasing a cat is a normal situation. But what if it was extremely hot outside? How would that affect the norm? The animals might be so exhausted from the heat that they would move much slower. They wouldn't change their normal action; they'd just change their pace.

The subject of the comparison should be familiar to a child. You may wish to brainstorm ideas in the following categories.

**People:** professional athletes, teachers, musicians, television personalities

**Places:** child's room, amusement park, swimming pool, beach, campground

**Emotions:** fear, anger, happiness, sadness

**Sensory experiences:** loud, quiet, bright, hot, cold, windy, dark

Examples:

*The basketball player jumped so high that he needed an oxygen mask.*

*Her room was so dirty that the flies moved out.*

*The music was so loud that he kept hearing it an hour after he turned it off.*

Remind students to create comparisons that respect the feelings of others and to use good judgment regarding subject matter. Humor should not be used as a cover for rudeness.

# Cross-Curriculum Uses

### Science

Students can make comparisons between two planets.
For example, *Jupiter is so large that it went on a diet and lost five hundred Plutos.*

### Social Studies

Students can make historical comparisons. There's even a pun in this example: *The ancient castles of Europe were so grand that one person couldn't visit all the rooms in a day—it also took several knights!*

### Additional Ideas

Challenge students to find similarities between two very different things. The answers don't have to be humorous. For example, *How are a fast-food hamburger and a paper bag similar?* (They are similar colors; some say they taste the same.) *How are a camera and an audiocassette similar?* (They allow you to record events; they are frequently made of plastic; they contain a long, ribbon-shaped storage medium.)

# WHATZITS??

## Value and Educational Applications

- Visual expression

- Brainstorming

- Creative thinking

# Writing Technique

Whatzits are simple drawings that at first look like a collection of random shapes. They actually represent a point of view or unusual perspective described by a humorous caption. The best way to understand whatzits is to look at a few.

You may see nothing but two abstract shapes in the picture to the right. The challenge of creating whatzits is to generate a humorous explanation.

Let's look at the picture again with an explanation beneath.

A close-up of two elephants rubbing noses.
A bird's-eye view of two dead-end roads.

The caption creates humor by establishing the point of view. Words such as *close-up* and *bird's-eye* allow the writer to create unique, often silly points of view.

Examples:

A close-up of a piece of shredded wheat surrounded by Cheerios.
A polka-dotted envelope with a stamp on it.

How toes look to a giant.
Two caterpillars meeting at the top of a hill.

A flying saucer about to crash.
A close-up of someone sticking his or her tongue out.
A hat for sleeping bats.

My whatzits usually start with a drawing. I'll often outline a frame, then draw random shapes inside. Usually my drawing generates a humorous idea. I'll play with the drawing—turning it upside down and sideways or redrawing it bigger or smaller—until something happens that makes me laugh.

Repeating a drawing several times often gives me an idea. Here is an example.

Three stepping stones in a dry lake.
Three buildings without windows.
Close-up of three unsharpened pencils.

Sometimes I just use a simple shape.

An unpopular balloon.
Bird's-eye view of a nail.

The explanations do not have to be logical. They have to make sense only in light of the drawing.

Once you have a drawing, ask yourself, "What could this be?" Pay attention to the wording here. I'm not asking, "What is this?" Like riddle writing, the idea is to write a funny setup. The drawing is the punch line, even though the reader sees it first. The challenge is to write a ridiculous context for the sketch.

# Cross-Curriculum Uses

### Science

- Have students create close-up and bird's-eye views of animals, plants, and science-related objects. Have classmates try to guess what the object is.

- Find and cut out photos or drawings of animals, plants, and other science-related objects. Glue or tape pictures to a piece of construction paper. Cut several holes in a second piece of construction paper. Make sure the holes are different sizes and shapes (see drawing below). Cover each hole with a self-stick note.

Remove the self-stick notes one by one and challenge students to identify the animal or object hiding beneath.

## Social Studies

Have students create a bird's-eye view of the Washington Monument, the Great Wall of China, or the Pyramids. Or students can create a fisheye view of Columbus's boats.

## Reading/Language Arts

Understanding a story's perspective, or point of view, is an important part of the writing process. Whatzits can help introduce how a changing point of view can lead to dramatic or humorous effects. Have students look for changes in perspective in the stories they're reading.

## Additional Ideas

Instead of having them draw shapes, encourage students to use geometric shapes of paper to create images and funny captions. If a computer drawing program is available, have one group of students create computer-generated shapes and another group write funny explanations.

# PUNS

## Value and Educational Applications

- Use of synonyms

- Creative thinking

- Proper and improper use of nouns

# Writing Technique

You can create a pun by replacing a word with a similar-sounding word that has a different meaning.

Examples:

*My pony has a cold.*
*Of course it has a colt. It's a little hoarse.*

*Where's Jennifer?*
*She went to the reptile farm.*
*Well, for goodness' snake!*

*Did you start the campfire?*
*Yes, now at last I'm flameous.*

You can use rhymes to create puns. Puns can also be based on words that relate in other ways, such as clichés. An expression such as *speak for yourself* can be modified for Halloween as *shriek for yourself.* Or maybe a burglar would tell his fellow burglar to *sneak for yourself.*

Puns often pop up during a normal conversation or passage in a story. While the technique used to create puns is similar to the one used to invent homophone riddles, it's the unexpected appearance that makes them different. Puns are best used when the listener or reader is taken by surprise.

# Cross-Curriculum Uses

### Science

Students can make puns on science terms.

For example, the word *reptiles* could generate puns based on the word *tiles*, as in *flooring tiles*. Or the word *reptile* could become *rep-tall*, as in *tall reptiles*.

### Social Studies

Students can make puns of historical places, persons, and events.
For example:

*We went to the capital of Italy and just "Romed" around.*

*Did you visit Beethoven's grave?*
*Yes, and he was sitting there erasing music.*
*They told us it was Beethoven decomposing.*

# CLICHÉS WITH A TWIST

## Value and Educational Applications

- Knowledge of folklore and folk sayings

- Familiarity with homophones and synonyms

- Proper and improper use of nouns

# Writing Technique

You can bet your bottom dollar that as sure as you're born you use clichés. Clichés serve as a kind of verbal shorthand that allows people to express themselves in familiar ways. By modifying a word or two within a cliché, a humor writer can create original, clever, and occasionally hilarious new phrases. Here are a few examples.

| Cliché | Cliché with a twist |
| --- | --- |
| *Six of one, a half-dozen of the others* | *Sick swan, a half-dozen of the otters* |
| *All's well that ends well.* | *All's whale that ends whale.* |
| *The status quo* | *The status crow* |
| *Lock, stock, and barrel* | *Lox stuck in barrels* |
| *Go for it!* | *Gopher it!* |
| *Hook, line, and sinker* | *Hawk, lion, and stinker* |
| *Boy meets girl* | *Boa meets gull* |

After you've practiced, you can create new clichés based on themes or categories. Here are some examples of "chicken" clichés with a twist.

| Cliché | Cliché with a twist |
| --- | --- |
| *Living in a fool's paradise* | *Living in a fowl's paradise* |
| *Poetry in motion* | *Poultry in motion* |
| *A chip off the old block* | *A chick off the old flock* |
| *Let the chips fall where they may.* | *Let the chicks fall where they may.* |
| *Fools rush in.* | *Fowls rush in.* |

Illustrating these clichés can be quite amusing.
*Poultry in motion* might look like this.

Use the bibliography to find books of clichés or make up your own
list. Then try to make some "twists" on the clichés. After you've
had some success, you might try proverbs and other familiar
phrases. Here are some examples.

| Proverb | Proverb with a twist |
|---|---|
| *A fool and his money are soon parted.* | *A fowl and his money are soon parted.* |
| *A rolling stone gathers no moss.* | *A rolling stone gathers no moths.* |
| *A half a loaf is better than none.* | *A heifer, loafers, butter, and nun.* |

Do you remember this famous line from the movie *My Fair Lady*? *The rain in Spain stays mainly in the plain.* You can make it funnier by "twisting" it, as in *The cranes in Spain stay mainly to complain.*

You can twist famous names too. Do you remember the beautiful bird whose face launched a thousand ships? That's right—it was *Heron of Troy!* Do you recall the name of the chicken that terrorized villages across Asia? Of course, it was *Atilla the Hen!*

Try your hand at twisting these phrases.

*Putting the cart before the horse*

*A receding hairline*

*The peasants are revolting*

*Ring around the rosies*

*Adding fuel to the fire*

*All roads lead to Rome*

*All the news that's fit to print*

*A clean bill of health*

*Ten-gallon hat*

*Head over heels*

# A Note From the Author

Each year I visit as many as one hundred schools and address a dozen or more regional and national educational conferences. I use these opportunities to talk with teachers and librarians about books they would like to see written and the creative ways they use the books they've purchased for the classroom. With this in mind, I'd like to invite you and your students to write to me. Let me know how you've used this book and what new and creative ways you've come up with to write fast and to write funny. If you'd like a personal response, please include a self-addressed, stamped envelope.

Mike Artell
P.O. Box 1819
Covington, LA 70434

# Bibliography

Ammer, Christine. *It's Raining Cats and Dogs.* Dell Publishing, 1989.

Artell, Mike. *The Wackiest Nature Riddles on Earth.* Sterling Publishing, 1992.

Brandreth, Gyles. *The Biggest Tongue Twister Book in the World.* Wings Books, 1992.

Brewton, Sara and John. *My Tongue's Tangled and Other Ridiculous Situations.* Crowell, 1973.

Charlton, James. *Bred Any Good Rooks Lately?* Doubleday, 1986.

Cunningham, Bonnie. *The Best Book of Riddles, Puns and Jokes.* Doubleday, 1979.

Hauptman, Don. *Cruel and Unusual Puns.* Dell Publishing, 1991.

Keller, Charles. *Ballpoint Bananas and Other Jokes for Kids.* Simon & Schuster Books for Young Readers, 1976.

Maestro, Giulio. *What's a Frank Frank? Tasty Homograph Riddles.* Clarion Books, 1984.

Moger, Art. *The Complete Pun Book* or *The Best Book of Puns.* Carol Publishing Group, 1981.

Mullins, Edward S. *The Big Book of Limericks.* Platt & Munk, 1969.

Rogers, James. *The Dictionary of Clichés.* Wings Books, 1992.

Schultz, Sam. *101 Knock-Knock Jokes Guaranteed to Make Even a Sourpuss Smile.* Lerner, 1982.

Young, Sue K. *The Scholastic Rhyming Dictionary.* Scholastic, 1994.